EPHESIANS AND PHILEMON

STUDIES IN THIS SERIES *Available from your Christian bookstore:*

ephesians and philemon

12 DISCUSSIONS FOR GROUP BIBLE STUDY

MARILYN KUNZ &
CATHERINE SCHELL

TYNDALE HOUSE
PUBLISHERS, INC.
WHEATON, ILLINOIS

Twelfth printing, October 1982
Library of Congress Catalog Card Number 73-81011
ISBN 0-8423-0695-1
Copyright © 1965 by Marilyn Kunz and Catherine Schell
Printed in the United States of America

contents

How to Use
This Discussion Guide

Each study guide in the Neighborhood Bible Study series is prepared with the intention that the ordinary adult group will, by using this guide, be able to rotate the leadership of the discussion. Those who are outgoing in personality are more likely to volunteer to lead first, but within a few weeks it should be possible for almost everyone to have the privilege of directing a discussion session. Everyone, including people new to the Bible who may not yet have committed themselves to Christ, should take a turn in leading by asking the questions from the study guide.

Reasons for this approach are:

1/ The discussion leader will prepare in greater depth than the average participant.

2/ The experience of leading a study stimulates a person to be a better participant in the discussions led by others.

3/ Members of the group which changes discussion leadership weekly tend to feel that the group belongs to everyone in it. It is not "Mr. or Mrs. Smith's Bible study."

4/ The Christian who by reason of spiritual maturity and wider knowledge of the Bible is equipped to be a spiritual leader in the group is set free to *listen* to everyone in the group in a way that is not possible when leading the discussion. He (she) takes his regular turn in leading as it comes around, but if he leads the first study in a series, he must guard against the temptation to bring a great deal of outside knowledge and source material which would make others feel they could not possibly attempt to follow his example of leadership.

For study methods and discussion techniques refer to the first booklet in this series, *How to Start a Neighborhood Bible Study,* as well as to the following suggestions.

How to participate in a study using this guide

1/ Read through the designated portion of the chapter in Ephesians daily during the week. Paul's letter to the Ephesians is so rich that it takes time to assimilate it into your thinking. Use it in your daily time of meditation and prayer, asking God to teach you what he has for you in it.

2/ Take two or three of the guide questions each day and try to answer them from the passage. Use these questions as tools to dig deeper into the passage. In this way you can cover all the guide questions before the group discussion.

3/ Use the summary questions to tie together the whole chapter in your thinking.

4/ *As an alternative* to using this study in your daily quiet time, spend at least two hours in sustained study once during the week using the above suggestions.

If you prepare well for each study session, you will find that these letters have much to challenge, strengthen and mature you in your spiritual life. If you are unwilling to prepare well, Ephesians in particular will seem confusing and difficult.

How to prepare to lead a study

1/ Follow the above suggestions on preparing to participate in a study. Pray for wisdom and the Holy Spirit's guidance.

2/ Familiarize yourself with the study guide questions until you can rephrase them in your own words if necessary to make you comfortable using them in the discussion.

3/ The first discussion, a survey of Ephesians, should require only one session. Some of the other studies may require two sessions. It is *not* recommended that you spend more than two sessions on one chapter. Each session should run from an hour to an hour and a half.

4/ Pray for the ability to guide the discussion with love and understanding.

How to lead a study

1/ Begin with prayer for minds open to understand and hearts willing to obey the Word of the Lord. You may ask another member of the group to pray if you have asked him ahead of time.

2/ Except during the first discussion, allow three to five minutes for members of the group to share what they learned through following the suggestions for practical action given at the end of the previous week's study.

3/ Have the Bible portion read aloud by paragraphs. Be sure to have the reading done by paragraph or thought units, *never* verse by verse. It is not necessary for everyone to read aloud, or for each to read an equal amount.

4/ Guide the group to discover what the passage says by asking the discussion questions. Use the suggestions from the section on "How to encourage everyone to participate."

5/ As the group discusses the Bible passage together, encourage each one to be honest in self-appraisal. You must take the lead in spiritual honesty. Try to avoid hypocrisy in any form.

6/ Allow time at the end of the discussion to answer the summary questions which help to tie the whole study together.

7/ Bring the discussion to a close at the end of the time allotted. Ask one of the group members to read the conclusion section. Then, as leader, give the practical suggestions to be followed during the coming week. Close in a prayer relevant to what has been discussed.

How to encourage everyone to participate

1/ Encourage discussion by asking several people to contribute answers to a question. "What do the rest of you think?" or "Is there anything else which could be added?" are ways of encouraging discussion.

2/ Be flexible and skip any questions which do not fit into the discussion as it progresses.

3/ Deal with irrelevant issues by suggesting that the purpose of your study is to discover what is *in the passage*. Suggest an informal chat about tangential or controversial issues after the regular study is dismissed.

4/ Receive all contributions warmly. Never bluntly reject what anyone says, even if you think the answer is incorrect. Instead ask in a friendly manner, "Where did you find that?" or "Is that actually what it says?" or "What do some of the rest of you think?" Allow the group to handle problems together.

5/ Be sure you don't talk too much as the leader. Redirect those questions which are asked you. A discussion should move in the form of an asterisk, back and forth between members, not in the form of a fan, with the discussion always coming back to the leader. The leader is to act as moderator. As members of a group get to know each other better, the discussion will move more freely, progressing from the fan to the asterisk pattern.

6/ Don't be afraid of pauses or long silences. People need time to think about the questions and the passage. Never, *never* answer your own question — either use an alternate question or move on to another area for discussion.

7/ Watch hesitant members for an indication by facial expression or bodily posture that they have something to say, and then give them an encouraging nod or speak their names.

8/ Discourage too talkative members from monopolizing the discussion by specifically directing questions to others. If necessary speak privately to the over-talkative one about the need for discussion rather than lecture in the group, and enlist his aid in encouraging all to participate.

Introduction to
Ephesians and Philemon

Paul's letter to the Ephesians has been called the "Queen of the Epistles" because of its outstanding devotional and theological content. It was one of four letters written by Paul while prisoner in Rome about A.D. 62 (See Acts 28:16, 30, 31.) The other three letters were Colossians, Philippians, and the personal note to Philemon.

In a number of manuscripts, the words "at Ephesus" in Ephesians 1:1 are omitted. This leads many scholars to believe that this letter was intended from the beginning for wider distribution than at Ephesus, perhaps that in each place the messenger bringing the letter would insert the words "at ____" appropriate for his listeners.

It is probable that this was a circular letter intended for the Gentile converts to Christianity throughout all Asia Minor. Ephesus was the chief city of the many cities of this province, and a place where Paul had spent over two years on his third missionary journey. For background on the church in Ephesus and the surrounding areas, read Acts 18:18 through 20:1, 17-38.

Discussion 1 / Ephesians 1:1 through 6:24

A Survey of the Letter

ADVANCE PREPARATION

The purposes of this survey study are to gain an overall view of the letter to the Ephesians and to understand the situation of the people to whom it was first written. Don't get bogged down in minute particulars in this first session. You will have ample opportunity to study each section of the letter in detail in the weeks ahead.

In preparation for this survey session, each person should read the whole letter in a recent translation at one sitting, trying to picture himself as a Christian of the first century reading this letter for the first time. Everyone should read the sections in Acts, chapters 18-20, about the coming of the gospel to Ephesus and the nearby parts of Asia Minor.

DISCUSSION QUESTIONS

1. At the beginning of the group discussion, ask one person to go through the letter reading aloud only the first verse or complete sentence of each paragraph.

For this reading use a paragraphed translation in contemporary English such as the New English Bible (NEB), Revised Standard Version (RSV), Good News for Modern Man — Today's English Version (TEV), The Living Bible (TLB), the Jerusalem Bible, or J. B. Phillips' New Testament in Modern English.

The rest of the group should listen rather than following in their Bibles. This will remind everyone of the main ideas of the letter.

2. What impressions do you get of Paul's purpose in writing this letter? What thoughts or ideas impressed you from reading it?

3. What differences do you observe between the first half of the letter (chapters 1-3) and the second half (chapters 4-6)? Why, do you think, didn't Paul put the contents of chapters 4-6 first?

4. Read aloud the first word or phrase of the following verses which are introductory to major sections of the letter: 1:15; 2:11; 3:1; 3:14; 4:1; 4:25; 5:1; 6:10. What do these phrases reveal about the type of writing here? If you were to write a letter to your son at college, using similar expressions, what kind of letter would you say you had written?

5. What does Paul tell about himself in this letter? See 1:1, 16; 3:1-4, 7-9, 13; 4:1; 6:19, 20. If this were your only source of information about Paul, what could you tell about who he was, his job, his situation as he wrote, his ambitions, etc.?

6. What does your preliminary survey of this letter reveal about those to whom it was addressed? What was their former state, their present position, the goal or direction they should be taking?

7. From the events relating to the formation and growth of the church at Ephesus detailed in Acts 18-20, what do you learn about the society of that day? Describe the pressures, concerns, and opportunities facing the Christians to whom Paul wrote this letter.

8. Imagine yourself as a first-century resident of Asia Minor, not a Christian, who has come upon this letter. From it what impressions do you get of Jesus Christ and of what it would mean to be his follower?

CONCLUSION

This letter was written to those whose lives had been drastically changed by their commitment to Jesus Christ as Lord and Savior. Paul was concerned that they appreciate the scope of God's plan in Jesus Christ, and that they live in the light of this. The letter to the Ephesians speaks not only of the destiny of the church, but also of the practical responsibilities of the individual Christian in every relationship of life.

Discussion 2 / Ephesians 1:1-14

The Purpose of God

"What is the meaning of life? What is the purpose of it all? I just work to eat, eat to live, and live to work — it seems pointless!" People need a purpose for living, a justification for existence. The Christian has such a reason for being which Paul spells out in this first section of his letter. Following the usual letter-writing pattern of his day, Paul begins with a salutation (verses 1, 2) followed by a thanksgiving (verses 3-14).

Ephesians 1:1, 2

1. How does the author of this letter describe himself? the source of his authority? (Note — *Apostle* means "one who is sent with a message.") Compare with Acts 22:6-16, especially verses 14, 15.

2. How does Paul describe those to whom this letter is addressed? Define *saints* and *faithful*. Note their spiritual location. (*In Christ Jesus* expresses the vital union and fellowship that exists between Christ and believers.)

3. Verse 2 combines the two forms of greeting used in their letters by the Greeks (*grace*) and by the Hebrews (*peace*). Define *grace* and *peace*. What is their source? What relationship is implied between these believers and God? between these believers and Jesus Christ?

4. Paul blesses God with words and thoughts for all with which God has blessed man in actions of love and undeserved favor. How many times in these verses does the phrase *in Christ* (or similar expressions) occur? List briefly each of the things God has done for the Christian in verses 3-14.

5. What choice did God make (verse 4)? When? For what purpose? Having chosen us, what relationship does God intend between us and himself (verse 5)? Why? Note the repetition of this phrase in verses 6, 12, 14. What has God done to bring us into this relationship (verses 7-9)?

6. Describe the gifts of God which come to those in Jesus Christ (verses 7, 8). What did it cost God to give these gifts? What do redemption and forgiveness mean for the person who receives them? (See Phillips' translation or the NEB.)

7. *Mystery* in the New Testament means something undiscoverable by human reason which has now been revealed by God. What mystery has God made known? What does the Christian understand to be the final goal of history? How is God's power over time and over the universe described (verses 9-11)?

8. What is the Christian's purpose in life (verse 12)? How should this affect practically our daily living?

9. What assurance does a Christian possess (verses 13, 14)? What steps precede such assurance (verses 12, 13)? What do the terms *truth* and *gospel* suggest about the Christian message?

10. A seal was a mark of ownership, a stamp of authenticity. What does it mean to be *sealed* with the promised Holy Spirit (verse 13)? Who owns the Christian now? Compare Acts 2:38; 10:47.

An *earnest* in business transactions in Paul's day meant a partial payment of the purchase money or land given as the seal of a contract, the pledge that full payment in kind would be made. Remembering this, what does it mean for the Christian that the Holy Spirit is the earnest (guarantee, pledge) of our inheritance? (What will be the nature of our future life in heaven? What confidence does the present possession of the Holy Spirit give us?)

11. How does Paul emphasize the unity of Jew and Gentile in Christ in verses 11-14? *We who first hoped in Christ* refers to Jews, *you also* to Gentiles, *we* (verse 14) to Jews and Gentiles in Christ. What is their common hope? Compare verse 14 and 1 Peter 1:3-5; Romans 8:18.

SUMMARY

1. What is God's ultimate purpose for the universe? What does a Christian already possess? To what can he look forward? What is the meaning of existence to the person in Christ?

2. What evidences are there in this section for the doctrine of the Trinity of God?

CONCLUSION

This passage is a hymn of praise describing God's purpose in history, to unite all things in Christ. This plan includes change and development in those whom God has chosen, including redemption, forgiveness, and insight into God's will until every Christian lives to the praise of God's glory. All of these things are accomplished in, through, and by our Lord Jesus Christ.

PRACTICAL SUGGESTIONS

Spend some time today considering the benefits that are yours in Christ as you have discovered them in Ephesians 1: 1-14. Look around you and study a tree, a cloud, a child, a man. Meditate on the meaning of Ephesians 1:10, thinking about what *all things* may include.

Discussion 3 / Ephesians 1:15 through 2:10

Alive in Christ

A frequent corruption of Christianity is the teaching that it is a religion of good works, that one's right standing with God depends upon doing good, upon working for one's salvation. That nothing could be further from the truth is made very clear in this section of Paul's letter.

Ephesians 1:15-23

1. Why does Paul pray for his readers? What is his first thought in prayer? To whom is his prayer addressed?

2. Paul prays that God will give these believers spiritual wisdom and insight to know more of him. In what particular area of knowledge does Paul pray that his readers will have wisdom and insight (verse 17)? What three specific facts (verses 18, 19) does Paul pray that these Christians may know?

3. What is the hope to which God has called us as Christians? Compare 1 Peter 5:10; Romans 8:18, 19, 23, 24.

4. In the Old Testament God called the people of Israel his own portion and inheritance (Deuteronomy 32:9). In what ways are Christians a rich and glorious inheritance to God? (John 14:23; 17:1, 6, 9, 10, 20-23)

5. What power for daily living is available to the Christian believer? Describe the scope of this power. What example of this power does Paul relate (verse 20)?

6. How should the knowledge that such vast resources of

power are available to you affect you in time of difficulty or trouble?

7. What position and authority does Christ now have? How is he described in relation to the Father? to all other powers and persons? to the whole universe? to the church?

8. Compare the relationship of Christ to the universe with the relationship of Christ to the church. In using the illustration of head and body, what truth does Paul point out about Christ and the church? (What type of union or interdependence of functions exists between the human head and body? For what functions is each necessary?)

Ephesians 2:1-10

9. List in two columns and note the contrasts between man's condition by nature (verses 1-3) and his position in Christ (verses 4-10). In what sense had Paul's readers once been dead? What loyalties had they formerly held? What actions had characterized them?

Read verses 1-3 in at least two contemporary translations. Note whom Paul includes in this former way of life.

10. What amazing change has been accomplished in these people to whom Paul writes? When? How? By whom? Why? In verses 5-8 what is referred to as past? as future? as present? Compare 2:4-6 with 1:19, 20.

11. What is taught here about the nature and purpose of our salvation (verses 8-10)? Although good works can never of themselves put us right with God, what place do they have in the Christian life?

12. Why is it wrong to try to earn salvation by good works? What does such thinking suggest about God? about man?

13. What do the terms *his workmanship* and *created in Christ Jesus* suggest as far as the Christian's taking credit for any of the good works he does after he becomes a Christian?

SUMMARY

1. What does Paul want his readers to know about Jesus Christ and about their relationship to him?

2. Into what two classifications does Paul divide all men in 2:1-10? How can a person move from one classification into the other?

3. What changes should take place in the one who becomes a Christian?

CONCLUSION

If Paul's prayers in 1:15-23 were answered in us, we would become keenly aware of our destiny, we would yearn to fulfill our calling, we would appreciate God's evaluation of our fellow Christians and the church. We would begin to act upon the power available to us as Christians. Most of all, we would realize the tremendous scope of the great salvation we possess through Jesus Christ, our Lord.

PRACTICAL ACTION

Memorize Ephesians 2:8-10. Have you ever accepted the free gift of God's mercy in Christ, or are you still working your own way to heaven? Look at the two columns you wrote in answer to question 9, and find to which category you belong.

Discussion 4 / Ephesians 2:11-22

Oneness in Christ

What are the things which divide people in our time? Consider the labels we use to separate people, such as liberal and conservative, black and white, rich and poor, management and labor, educated and illiterate, upper class, middle class, lower class. The tragedy is that sometimes these labels divide members of the Christian church. Although dealing specifically with the cleavage between Jew and Gentile, this passage gives reasons against accepting any divisions between Christians.

(This study may require two discussion sessions. If so, it is suggested that you end the first session with question 8.)

Ephesians 2:11-22

1. In what terms does Paul identify his readers (verse 11)? Who were the *circumcision?* the *uncircumcision?*

Note — Circumcision was the sign of God's covenant with Israel, the seal that they were God's people. See Genesis 17: 7-14.

2. What does Paul want his readers to remember about their former state before God raised them to new life in Christ? Before Christ came, what advantages did the Jews have in comparison to the Gentiles (verses 11, 12)?

3. Note the progression of thought in verse 12. "No hope of a Messiah . . . aliens from the society whose king was God . . . strangers who did not possess God's promises . . . without

hope . . . without God." What is the climax of thought here? Why is it the logical conclusion to the conditions described? What does it mean to you to say that someone is *without God?*

4. How does a person's concept of Jesus Christ and a person's relationship to him affect his view of the meaning of life? his view of the direction of history?

5. For the covenant promises possessed by Israel (verse 12), see Exodus 6:6-8; Deuteronomy 28:9-15.

6. Notice the number of times that *peace* and *one* appear in verses 14-18. Before Christ came, Jew and Gentile were separated by a mutual animosity and contempt (verse 14), by an actual wall beyond which the Gentile could not go into the inner areas of the temple in Jerusalem (verse 14), and by God's commandments which the Jews possessed and the Gentiles did not (verse 15). How did Christ break down these barriers and bring peace between Jew and Gentile? How must both Jew and Gentile now come to God?

7. List all the things accomplished in Christ for the Gentile (those *far off*), and for the Jew (those *near*), verses 13-17. How were these things accomplished (verses 13, 15, 16, 18)?

8. In what sense did Christ abolish the law of commandments and ordinances (verse 15)? See Romans 10:4; Acts 15:1, 6-11; Galatians 3:23-26; Ephesians 2:8-10; Mark 15:37, 38; Hebrews 10:19, 20.

9. What was the twofold purpose of Christ's work for both Jew and Gentile (verses 15b, 16, 18)?

10. What do Christian believers of divergent backgrounds (whether of culture, race, or color) have in common? See 2:8-10, 13, 18. In view of what it cost Jesus Christ to unite men of opposing backgrounds to one another and to God, what should be our attitude toward any continuing hostility between those who are now Christians? What practical steps can we take to learn to accept and love one another?

11. Since Christ has destroyed the barriers between Jew and Gentile and between them and God, what are the consequences (results) in the situation of all Christians (verses 19-22)?

12. Paul uses the terms of citizenship (verse 19), of family

(19), and of a building (20-22) to describe the equality of privilege which Gentile Christians have with Jewish Christians. When a person becomes a citizen of a country what new privileges, loyalties, and responsibilities are his? What happens to a person who becomes part of a household or family?

13. In comparing these Christian believers to a temple being constructed, what important points does Paul teach about the church? Upon what does the unity of the whole structure depend?

Upon what other foundation do people sometimes try to establish the church? Why? Notice also in verse 21 that the word *grows* is used. What does this tell you about this temple?

14. What is the purpose of this temple?

SUMMARY

1. Why did Christ die? How should understanding the meaning of Christ's death upon the cross affect our relationships with other Christians? Why must a Christian never put up a barrier between himself and another who is in Christ?

2. What are the barriers in the Christian church which many today accept as normal? Practically speaking, what should we do about them? Remember the key phrase in verse 13, *in Christ Jesus*.

3. What privilege do we possess which surpasses even that of fellowship with other Christians (verses 18, 22)? If we exercise this privilege of access into God's presence, what should happen as a natural consequence in our relations with other Christians?

CONCLUSION

God's exclusiveness consists in planning everything in and through Jesus Christ. Man's exclusiveness consists in choosing secondary factors and making them primary in the church. In our day we see much of the organized church acting as if the second chapter of this letter had never been written.

PRACTICAL ACTION

Prepare your favorite recipe or make something in your workshop. As you work, observe the changes taking place in what you are making. Think about the changes which have taken place in your own life as you have trusted yourself to Jesus Christ. Write down these changes.

Discussion 5 / Ephesians 3:1-21

Paul's Calling and Prayer

The Christian church frequently comes under attack from outsiders, yet confusion from within the church as to her true message and purpose has been more devastating to her well-being. In this chapter Paul speaks of his own commission and the ministry of the church in the plan of God. He goes on to pray for the Gentile Christians, and to praise God.

Ephesians 3:1-13

1. As he wrote this letter, Paul was a prisoner in Rome awaiting trial before Nero. Nevertheless, how did Paul define his situation? What does this indicate about Paul's view of life? How do you evaluate your own negative circumstances? How must Paul's point of view have made all the difference to him in this experience?

2. Note the repetition of the phrase *for this cause* (*reason*) in verses 1, 14, indicating that verses 2-13 are a digression in thought from what Paul started out to say. What thought in verse 1 sidetracks Paul? To what mystery does he refer? Compare Ephesians 1:9, 10 with 3:4, 6. Note that Paul moves from a general statement in 1:9, 10 to specific details in 3:6.

3. Put into your own words the three statements Paul makes concerning the Gentile Christians in 3:6. Contrast with their former state in 2:11, 12. What has brought about such a change in the condition of these people? Compare 2:13 and 3:6.

4. How did Paul come to understand God's plan for the Gentile world (verses 2-6)? For whom is this revelation intended? What is Paul's purpose in preaching (verse 9)?

Note — Erdman comments that the *unsearchable riches of Christ* (verse 8) are "the infinite greatness of all that wealth of wisdom and knowledge, of beauty and power, of sympathy and love, that are in Christ Jesus our Lord . . . an infinite store which none can exhaust."

5. In spite of all his privileges and responsibilities, how does Paul view himself? What effects would Paul's humility have upon his work for Christ? upon his attitude toward those he served (verse 13)?

6. What is the place of the church in God's plan (verse 10)? How was God's eternal plan accomplished (verse 11)? What is the result for Christians (verse 12)? Compare 2:18. Why is access to God essential for man? If we realize that sending the gospel to all nations was not an afterthought but part of God's eternal purpose in Christ, what practical effect will this have on our proclamation of the gospel?

Ephesians 3:14-21

7. The ordinary Jewish position for prayer was to stand with outstretched hands, palms upward. To bow the knee meant to prostrate oneself in prayer before God. What does this position indicate as to the intensity of Paul's concern in prayer?

8. Paul resumes the statement he began in verse 1. What is the reason or cause for his prayer (2:19-22; 3:6)?

9. Read carefully Paul's prayer (verses 14-19). To whom does Paul address his prayer? What do you learn about God the Father from references thus far in Ephesians (1:2, 3, 17; 2:18; 3:15)? What confidence would the fatherhood of God described in verse 15 give to Paul in praying for these Gentile believers?

10. List Paul's petitions, rephrasing them in your own words. How are the needs of the inner man met?

Note — The Greeks used the phrase *the inner man* to include a man's reason, conscience, and will. The *heart* was not only the seat of a man's affections but of his intelligence and will.

11. How does Paul emphasize the vastness of the love of Christ? In whose company does a person come to understand the love of Christ (verse 18)? Why cannot the love of Christ ever be fully known?

12. Compare what is said about the church in 2:22 with what Paul prays for the individual Christian in 3:19. What must be the goal of the individual and of the church?

Note — *The fulness of God* includes all of God's excellencies and perfections. It refers to the moral qualities of God embodied in Jesus Christ which are increasingly communicated to believers and expressed in them as Christ dwells in their hearts by faith.

13. Compare the doxology (verses 20, 21) with which Paul concludes the first half of his letter with the doxology in Jude 24, 25. Why is God to be praised? Try to put verses 20, 21 into your own words. For the extent of *the power at work within us* see Ephesians 1:19, 20 and Jude 24.

14. How does God receive glory in the church? How does God receive glory in Christ? For how long? See also Ephesians 1:5, 6, 12; 3:10.

SUMMARY

1. What mystery does Paul discuss in Ephesians 3? What responsibility does Paul have in relation to this mystery?

2. From his prayer for his readers, what seems to be Paul's primary concern in writing this letter?

3. From what you have studied thus far in Ephesians, describe what Paul seems to have in mind when he uses the word *church* (3:10, 21).

CONCLUSION

Paul's intention in chapter 3 is to tell his Gentile Christian readers what he prays for them, but he pauses to describe his mission to make known to all nations the fact that salvation in Christ has been planned from eternity to include the Gentiles as well as the Jews. Both this parenthesis in verses 2-13 and Paul's prayer in verses 14-21 give us rich insights into the heart and mind of the apostle. What we pray for another reveals not only our highest hopes and concerns for him but also a great deal about ourselves.

PRACTICAL ACTION

We often think to pray only for the physical needs of those we love. Keep in mind what Paul prayed for the Christians of his day, and spend time each day this week praying specifically for the spiritual needs of the people for whom you are concerned.

List briefly in the space below Paul's requests on behalf of the Ephesians, putting them into your own words if you can. Then use them in your own prayers for others.

Discussion 6 / Ephesians 4:1-16

Christian Unity

With this chapter Paul begins the second half of his letter, calling upon his readers to express what they believe in the way they live. In chapters 4-6 he deals primarily with the practical applications to daily life of the great doctrines set forth in chapters 1-3. Paul exhorts each member of the church of Jesus Christ to so live that the whole church may fulfill God's plan and purpose for her. All things are to be united in Christ Jesus, and the church is to be Christ's instrument for bringing unity and harmony into the world.

Ephesians 4:1-6

1. What is the *calling* to which Paul's readers have been called (verse 1)? By saying *therefore* Paul refers us back to what he has stated previously concerning this calling. See especially 1:4-6, 11, 12; 2:10, 13, 19-22; 3:10, 20, 21.

2. State Paul's plea (verse 1) in your own words. Paul is in prison for the cause of Christ, in fact because of his ministry to the Gentiles. What effect should Paul's reminder of his imprisonment have upon his readers? From whom are you most likely to accept spiritual challenge?

3. With what four virtues (verse 2) does Paul describe a life worthy of the name Christian?

4. What knowledge about oneself leads to *lowliness* (*humility*) (verse 1)? See 2:1-3, 12, 13.

5. How does meekness (gentleness) differ from humility?

Note — Meekness does not mean weakness, but rather having every thought, desire, word and action under perfect control. Barclay comments that the meek man is one "who is so God-controlled that he is always angry at the right time but never angry at the wrong time; he is a man in whom self has died and whose whole life is directed and controlled by God."

6. What do longsuffering and forbearing (verse 2) mean? Note Romans 2:4; 2 Peter 3:15 for how we have benefited from this virtue. Give a practical example of forbearance in a Christian's life. See also Matthew 18:21, 22.

7. What connection do humility, meekness, and patience have with the expression of love for one's fellow Christians?

8. When a man walks in humility, meekness, patience, and love, what will result (verse 3)? Note that in verse 3 Paul emphasizes the *maintenance* of unity rather than the *achievement* of unity. What is the nature of the unity to which Paul refers?

9. How does Paul emphasize the fact that the unity about which he speaks is not man-made but of the Spirit of God (verses 4-6)? What are seven specific aspects of the unity which already exists among Christians? What part does the Trinity play in this?

Note — *One body* refers to the church. See Ephesians 1: 22, 23.

10. What is *the one hope of your calling,* the goal to which Christians are proceeding? See 1 Peter 1:3-5. *Faith* (verse 5) speaks of complete surrender to Jesus Christ. What is the essential meaning of Christian baptism? See Romans 6:3, 4.

11. What truth does Paul bring out about unity by emphasizing the fact that God is the Father of all believers, rather than speaking here of him as the King or the Judge? What else does verse 6 add to the understanding of this unity about which Paul speaks?

Ephesians 4:7-16

12. What diversity exists alongside of the unity just de-

scribed? What has been Paul's personal experience of such grace? See 3:2, 7-9.

13. What is the source of the talents and abilities (gifts) which individual Christians possess (verses 7-9)? How does remembering this fact help us to keep the humility of verse 2? Compare Romans 12:3, 6.

14. What are the gifts in verses 11, 12? What is the purpose (verse 12) behind this diversity of gifts? What is the ultimate goal of this ministry or service (verse 13)?

15. What is the difference between the unity already a reality in Christians (verses 3-7) and the unity for which we are to strive (verses 13-16)? How is the first to be guarded and how is the second to become a reality?

16. What weakness of childhood does Paul use to illustrate spiritual immaturity (verse 14)? How may we avoid being unstable Christians? Compare verse 14 with Galatians 1:6, 7. What picture is given of Christian maturity (verses 15, 16)? Why is Christian maturity never an individual matter? Why is each part of the body of Christ important?

SUMMARY

1. Describe how the individual Christian is to behave toward other Christians. What practical connection does this behavior have with the unity of the church?

2. What provisions has God made for the growth of Christians to spiritual maturity? Evaluate your own local church as to how effective it is in helping its individual members become like Christ.

3. Which individuals within your church possess the spiritual gifts mentioned in 3:11? To what extent are you participating in the work of your church to bring everyone in it to spiritual maturity?

CONCLUSION

The oneness of the Church is such a reality to Paul that he likens it to a complex living organism with interdependent members which must work in harmony with one another to function properly. The head of this living body is Christ who initiates, directs, and rules the activities of the whole body.

PRACTICAL ACTION

Listen carefully to a piece of music played by a symphony orchestra. Notice the importance of proper participation by each instrument in order to produce harmony and beauty. Consider your own function in the Christian fellowship. Are you playing your part properly?

Discussion 7 / Ephesians 4:17-32

The Old and the New

To live a new life different from the old is obligatory for every Christian. The change from the old life to the new would be particularly dramatic and obvious in those who had come out of the practices of the pagan world of Paul's time.

Ephesians 4:17-24

1. Put into your own words Paul's solemn command to his Christian readers. What terrible things characterize those who are outside of Christ (verses 17-19)? What is the Gentiles' relationship to God? Why? What is their resultant attitude toward sin? Compare verses 17-19 with Romans 1:21-25. What points are emphasized in both sections?

2. Give instances of people today who have done evil for so long that they no longer recognize it as wrongdoing. What modern evidence is there that men's hearts and minds can become ineffective in controlling their actions, so that they abandon themselves completely to every sort of evil? Give examples of people leading others to destruction for their own gratification.

3. What is set in contrast to the old life (verses 20, 21)? What three commands does Paul give (verses 22-24)? What are the differences between the old nature and the new nature? Compare verse 23 with Romans 8:5 and 12:2. What do these verses indicate as to how the process of renewal takes place? What part does the mind play in our actions?

4. How does Paul elaborate here upon his command in verse 22? What specific reasons are given for this reformation of conduct? How do these reasons bear out the theme of the whole epistle, namely, God's plan to unite all things in Christ? What actions are to take the place of those things which are put away?

5. What happens in a society or in a group where deception is practiced and a man's word can not be relied upon? How may we lie by silence as well as by speech?

6. Since Christians are members of the same body, what will happen if different parts of that body do not speak the truth to one another? (Compare to what happens to a human body when true messages are not relayed from one part to another, for example, when the hand touches a hot stove but the nerves transmit no message or the message that the stove is cool.)

7. What place does anger have in the Christian life? When is anger wrong for the Christian (verses 26, 27)? Compare Mark 3:4, 5; 11:15-17. What practices are to be followed in regard to anger? Note verses 26, 27 in Phillips' translation and in the NEB.

8. Why ought the converted thief to turn from stealing to honest work (verse 28)? In contrast why does the business world recommend hard work? What examples of thievery do we have in respectable society today?

9. When is talk evil? When is it edifying? Give examples of conversation which discourages or corrupts, of conversation which encourages, purifies, strengthens.

10. How could a Christian grieve the Holy Spirit? How does a child grieve his parents? Compare verse 30 and 1:13, 14 as to the importance of the Holy Spirit.

11. Contrast verses 31 and 32. Give examples of each of the wrong things which are to be put away. Instead of such attitudes, what is to characterize our actions and attitudes toward another person? What is the standard set for us?

SUMMARY

1. From what you have learned in this study, describe the non-Christian society of Paul's day. How did it differ from the non-Christian society of our own day? What effects of sin were evident in mind and heart and body?

2. How did Jesus Christ treat us? Because of this, and because we are fellow members of the body of Christ, how ought we as Christians to treat one another?

CONCLUSION

Our new life in Christ should be manifested by new conduct and new character. The change should be as evident as a new suit of clothes. Certain practices must be abandoned as unsuitable for a follower of Christ. We should, in fact, begin to treat each other as Jesus Christ has treated us.

PRACTICAL ACTION

To find out the thinking of your family, raise these questions at the dinner table some night this week: "What actions and attitudes, do you think, should characterize a Christian? How should a Christian be different from other people?"

Discussion 8 / Ephesians 5:1-20

Light and Darkness

Man by nature is a mimic. Through imitating his elders a child learns to walk, to talk, to eat properly, and to function in the culture in which he is growing up. Paul says that the Christian should copy or imitate God as a child does his father.

Ephesians 5:1-20

1. In what particular area is Paul concerned that Christians should imitate God? What example does he give to help them understand the quality of love about which he speaks? See also Romans 5:6-8.

2. Divide a sheet of paper into two columns and entitle them *darkness* and *light*. From verses 3-20 list in these colums the thoughts, words, and actions which characterize the old life and the new life.

3. Define fornication, uncleanness, and covetousness (verse 3). Why are these three linked together? What moral darkness surrounded the early Christians? See Romans 1:26-32.

4. What standard does Paul raise for the conduct and conversation of Christians? What harm is there in dirty stories, coarse talk, or flippancy of speech?

5. What two reasons does Paul give in verses 5, 6 for his clear command in verse 3? Why is a covetous man called an idol worshiper?

6. What verdict do verses 5, 6 pass upon the so-called "new morality" of our day? Into what sort of thinking con-

cerning immorality, impurity and covetousness are people today being deceived (verse 6)? By whom?

The "new morality" says that any sexual acts are all right
as long as they are meaningful and hurt no one, that "love" as
a motive makes any act legitimate.

7. What actions, negative and positive, should the Christian take (verses 7-11)? What reasons are given?

8. By using the term *light* (verses 8-10), what truths does
Paul emphasize? (Remember that light is necessary for physical life and growth, that light reveals the true nature of things,
that light shows up the bad for what it is, that light conquers
disease.

9. How can we expose our attitudes and actions to the
light of Christ (verse 13)? See John 8:12; 1 John 2:3, 6, 10.

10. Verse 14 is probably a quotation from an early Christian hymn, perhaps a baptismal hymn. What promise does it
give to those who become Christians?

11. What exhortations does Paul give in verses 15-20?
What gives Paul his sense of urgency (verse 16)? Give practical examples of wise and unwise uses of time and opportunities.

12. Verses 18-20 contrast two patterns of social life. What
is the stimulus and the result of each? What does it mean to
be *filled with the Spirit?* What practices, attitudes, and relationships result from being filled with the Spirit?

SUMMARY

1. Find the three major characteristics of the Christian life
as related in this passage using the expression *walk*. See
verses 2, 8, 15. What does each expression teach about the
whole direction and pattern of life for the Christian?

2. Observe the major contrasts in this passage: light and
darkness, wise and foolish, love and immorality, levity and
thanksgiving, filled with wine and filled with the Spirit. Put
into your own words the differences between these things.

3. How is it possible to live the life pleasing to God?

CONCLUSION

The standard of conduct befitting a Christian is so high that it can be compared with imitating God. Our Lord Jesus Christ in his Sermon on the Mount said, "You, therefore, must be perfect, as your heavenly Father is perfect." But how? It seems so difficult, so far beyond our strength. At the close of his letter Paul will tell his readers of the equipment available for them to live such a life, to fight such a battle.

PRACTICAL ACTION

In this passage Paul warns Christians against covetousness and greed, and urges us to exercise wisdom in order to understand the will of the Lord. When you have a few minutes alone, take your wallet (or your bankbook) and think prayerfully about whether your money is really under the control of God. Can you honestly give your material wealth to the Lord for him to direct its use?

Discussion 9 / Ephesians 5:21 through 6:9

Specific Relationships

The position of women and children has never been secure in a non-Christian world. In Paul's day, absolute power over the child lay in the hands of the father, even when the child became an adult. It was almost the automatic thing to drown a sickly child, and girl babies frequently were left to die. Even today in India, though it is against the law, parents may cut out the tongue of a child or otherwise deform children to make them more effective beggars. In the United States hospitals are coming to recognize the "battered child" syndrome.

Ephesians 5:21-33

1. How does verse 21 serve both as a suitable conclusion to the previous paragraph (verses 15-20) and a comprehensive introductory statement for the new section (5:21—6:9)? What does it mean to *submit* or *be subject* to another? Why should Christians do this?

2. Why should we not look for characteristics in our fellow Christians which make them worthy of our submission to them before we obey this command?

3. What three basic relationships are dealt with in 5:21—6:9? Consider how these relationships continue all our lives in one form or another at home, at school, at work.

4. To what relationship does Paul compare marriage? What was Christ's motive and what were his purposes in his sacrificial death for the church (verses 26, 27)? What is the rea-

on for Christ's continuing care for the church (verses 29, 30)? What is the church's response to Christ (verse 24)? Keep these truths in mind as you consider the commands to wives and husbands.

5. What are the responsibilities of a wife to her husband (verses 22-24, 33)? What do these verses mean in practical living? Is a wife never to disagree with her husband?

6. What responsibilities does a husband have to his wife? What kind of love is he to have for her? See verses 25-33. Why is it the husband rather than the wife who is directed to exercise this sacrificial, purifying, caring, unbreakable love? What is the opposite of each of these qualities of love? Who is the husband's example of such love?

Note that if husband and wife obey the commands directed to them, each one makes it easier for the other to fulfill his or her responsibilities in the relationship.

7. What other loyalties become secondary for husband and wife? How is the wife protected from tyranny by the commands given to the husband? Noting the purposes of Christ's love for his church, what are to be the aims of a husband's sacrificial and protecting love for his wife (verses 26, 27)?

8. What does it mean for a husband to love his wife as he loves himself? On the other hand, what happens to the marriage relationship when a husband regards his wife as an unpaid housekeeper and baby sitter?

9. To what does Paul liken the unity between man and wife (verses 31, 32)? What does this imply about the quality of the marriage bond and the stability of the relationship? How do verses 28, 31 substantiate this?

Ephesians 6:1-4

10. What is the first commandment a child should be taught? What does *in the Lord* mean? What promise accompanies the keeping of this command? How is honor shown in practical ways? Why, do you think, are both father and mother specifically mentioned?

11. Why is the warning in verse 4 addressed particularly to fathers? Compare Colossians 3:21. *Provoke* can also be

translated *overcorrect*. What positive responsibility does a father have to his children? What happens to the child whose father relinquishes this responsibility?

12. What effects do continual nagging, scolding, and criticism have upon children? How can parents know the proper balance of discipline? See Ephesians 5:1, 2; James 1:5.

Ephesians 6:5-9

13. Paul wrote in the context of the widespread slavery of his day when a slave was the absolute property of his master with no rights whatever. How would you apply Paul's commands for slaves and masters to employer-employee relationships today?

Put into your own words Paul's commands as they would affect: a factory assembly-line worker, a garage mechanic, a doctor, nurse, lawyer, businessman, store clerk, cleaning woman, and garbage collector. What temptations do *you* face in your work to be a "men-pleaser" or to do "eye-service"?

14. What perspective are employers to keep in regard to their position? How would a proper recognition of each one's responsibility to God help employers and employees in working out problems of labor contracts?

SUMMARY

1. How has the status of women, children, and servants been changed by Christianity?

2. Consider the simple duties and the sublime motives to which Paul directs his readers in this passage. Suggest some practical ways we can convey these to our children and young people.

3. What does Paul expect to see as evidence of Christ's rule in personal relationships between Christians?

4. What facts does this passage bring out about the relationship between Christ and his church?

CONCLUSION

In an affluent society where statistics indicate a high percentage of disturbed children and distressed wives, it becomes obvious that physical comforts and luxuries have not been satisfactory substitutes for responsible fathers and loving husbands. The commands given in this passage for the Christian at home and at work lay the foundation for spiritual and mental health and sound personal relationships.

PRACTICAL ACTION

During the coming week pray daily that God will help you to see and to carry out your responsibilities as a husband or wife, as a child and/or parent, as a servant and/or master. Concentrate on obeying Christ's commands to you in these relationships, whether others are doing so or not.

Discussion 10 / Ephesians 6:10-24

The Christian's Equipment

Paul was keenly aware of the spiritual battle in which every Christian is constantly engaged. Those who seek to enter into the enjoyment of the spiritual blessing of Ephesians 1:3 and who try to put into practice the life described in Ephesians 4:1—6:9 soon come to realize that such a life can only be lived by the enabling power of the Holy Spirit.

Ephesians 6:10-24

1. Contrast the atmosphere of this section with that of 5:21—6:9. What change of scene do you observe? What further dimension does Paul reveal in his concept of the Christian life? Why is spiritual conflict a continuing reality in the life of a Christian?

2. What commands does Paul give in verses 10, 11? Note the three major resources of the Christian suggested here. What armor is suitable for the Christian facing spiritual battle? Consider the illustration in 1 Samuel 17:38-40, 45-47.

3. What is revealed about the nature and sphere of action of the Christian's enemies (verses 11-16)? What methods of the enemy are particularly mentioned (verses 11, 16)? Compare 1 Peter 5:8.

What emphasizes the fact that this is a spiritual warfare, not a physical one, and that our enemies are not fellow human beings?

4. What does the expression *therefore take* (verse 13)

suggest about the Christian's preparation for spiritual conflict? What difference would there be if Paul had said, "Therefore make"? Who is responsible for the Christian's supplies in this battle?

5. Why is the Christian urged to take *God's* armor? What promise is implied (verse 13) to the one who does avail himself of this equipment? For the meaning of *the evil day* of which Paul speaks, read verse 13 in several different translations.

6. What parts of the body are specifically mentioned (verses 14-17)? What provision is made for each? Which part of the equipment is for defense? Which is for offense?

7. Why is truth (an awareness of the real facts about ourselves and about God) essential for success in spiritual battles? How can a soldier be hindered by not knowing the truth?

8. What vital organs of the body will the breastplate (verse 14) protect? Righteousness here means moral integrity. How can a life devoted to obeying God's will be a protection against spiritual attacks? How does a guilty conscience weaken us spiritually?

9. Every soldier knows the importance of good footwear. Compare verse 15 with Romans 10:15 and Isaiah 52:7. Why does the gospel of peace form a part of this armor for spiritual warfare?

10. What importance does Paul put upon the shield as a part of the Christian's equipment? How is faith the Christian's chief means of protection? From what? See also James 1:14; 1 Peter 2:11.

11. Give examples in which a Christian's close personal relationship with Christ through faith becomes a protecting shield for him against temptation. Compare 1 Corinthians 10:13.

12. The verb translated *take* in verse 17 means to *accept,* to *receive* the salvation God has provided for us of forgiveness for past sins and present deliverance from sin's power. Why does the head need special protection? What attacks might be made on the Christian through his mind? How does the assurance of our salvation equip us against such attacks?

13. What is the one weapon of offense necessary for the Christian? How may it be used defensively as well? Whose sword is it? Compare with Matthew 4:1-11 to see how Jesus used this weapon.

14. Compare the importance of the soldier's contact with headquarters with the commands regarding prayer in verses 18-20. For whom should prayer be made? Why?

15. How does a realization that others also are involved in this battle give us courage and perspective in our personal fight?

16. What is Paul's special request for prayer? With what assurance does Paul conclude his letter (verses 21, 22)? What responsibility does Tychicus have?

17. Compare verses 23, 24 with 1:1, 2. What is the meaning of Paul's benediction?

SUMMARY

1. What experiences have you had that make you aware of the reality of the spiritual battle in which Christians are engaged? In what specific ways have you found the armor of God effective?

2. How can we make sure that we don't go about unequipped or only partially equipped?

CONCLUSION

Although a great deal is expected of the Christian, sufficient resources are provided in Jesus Christ to enable him to meet all the demands placed upon him.

PRACTICAL ACTION

Ignore your favorite magazine or television program this week and do some reading which will be of spiritual value to you. Borrow a missionary biography from your church library. As you read it, watch for the spiritual battle and equipment of Ephesians 6.

ASSIGNMENT FOR NEXT WEEK

The next discussion will be a review of the whole letter. Before leaving today's session the group should read carefully through all eight review questions and make their choices of who will prepare which question(s) during the week.

Discussion 11 / Review of Ephesians 1 through 6

The aim of this review is to stimulate everyone in the group to read the whole letter thoughtfully again, alert to the major lines of thought (which are pointed out by the review questions).

Each member of the group should choose one or more of the review questions for special study and prepare to share his findings in the group discussion. Be sure that all of the review questions are covered by these individual choices.

Some questions will take longer to present to the group than others. However, if everyone has prepared his own question(s) well enough to share the answer with the group in his own words, using a written summary if he wishes, the review session will prove both helpful and interesting to all.

1. Summarize all that this letter teaches about the church including:
   —the relationship between Christ and the church
   —what the church of Christ already is
   —what the church is to become
   —the qualities that should characterize the life cf the whole church
   —God's provisions for the needs of the church
   —God's purpose through the church

2. Define the "mystery" of which Paul speaks in this letter. How did God deal with the separation between Jew and Gentile?

3. What changes take place in the life of an individual who comes to Christ? How is salvation obtained? What part do good works play in the Christian's experience?

4. Describe the work of Jesus Christ as presented in this letter.

5. What does this letter teach about the Trinity of God? Find references to the specific activities of Father, Son, and Holy Spirit, especially in accomplishing man's redemption. Note references not only to the Trinity of the Persons but to the Unity of the Godhead and the oneness of the will of God.

6. Describe how a Christian should live in society. What practices of life does he reject? choose?

7. Describe the Christian household. What is to characterize every relationship? Summarize the teaching given to husbands and wives, children and parents, servants and masters.

8. What is the Christian's purpose in life as revealed in this letter?

PRACTICAL ACTION

Choose a section of this letter that has been particularly meaningful to you. Using a hymnal, find a hymn which expresses the same thought. Memorize this hymn and share it with someone else.

Discussion 12 / Philemon

Love in Action

This letter apparently was written at the same time as the epistles to the Ephesians and the Colossians. All three letters were probably delivered by Tychicus who was accompanied by Onesimus. (Compare Colossians 4:7-9 and Ephesians 6: 21.)

This is a private letter and as such gives insight into Paul's personal life, revealing his own reactions in handling a specific problem. It is a shining example of how the truths of Paul's letter to the Ephesians were applied by him in the ordinary life of his day. The letter to Philemon was written on behalf of Onesimus, a runaway slave who had become a Christian through Paul's ministry in Rome.

Philemon

1. What do you learn about Philemon and his family (verses 1, 2)?
2. Compare verse 3 with Ephesians 1:2. Why is this Paul's customary greeting to his fellow Christians?
3. For what is Paul thankful? For what does he pray? What sort of relationship is evident between Paul and Philemon? What had Philemon already proven about himself as a Christian?
4. What is Paul's request of Philemon? On what basis does Paul make his appeal? Of what does he remind Philemon (verses 1, 9, 13)? How does Paul feel about Onesimus? Why?

5. What change has come over Onesimus? Why does Paul want to keep him in Rome, and why doesn't he do so? What risk is Paul taking in sending Onesimus back to Philemon? What is the cost to Onesimus? What fears might Paul and Onesimus have?

Remember the position of slaves in that day — they were regarded as living tools, not as persons, and a master had the legal right to punish or kill a slave for any misdeed as he might choose.

6. What is Paul asking from Philemon in verses 15-17? Why doesn't he ask Philemon to release Onesimus from slavery? Why doesn't Paul speak of the evils of slavery? How is he really asking more from Philemon than if he were to ask for physical release of his slave?

7. What indicates the probability that Onesimus has taken money from his master? (Consider the distance between Philemon's home, Colossae in Asia Minor, and Rome where Onesimus met Paul.) What is Paul prepared to do on Onesimus' behalf (verses 18, 19)?

8. How does Paul apply further pressure on Philemon in verses 19b-21? Why? Consider the social customs and pressures which Philemon is being asked to disregard. Compare this practical situation with Paul's teachings in Ephesians 4:1-3, 31, 32; 6:5-10.

9. What expectation does Paul have about Philemon as he writes? What does this indicate as to the sort of person Philemon is? What hope does Paul have about his own imprisonment? How would the expectation of Paul's arrival affect Philemon's decision about Onesimus?

10. In the light of the nature of this letter, what effect would verses 23, 24 have upon Philemon? Who else would be looking to Philemon for suitable Christian action in this matter?

SUMMARY

1. Describe the drama of joy and sorrow behind this brief letter. What did it mean for each of the three principals involved: Paul? Onesimus? Philemon?

2. How does this letter illustrate the putting into practice of Christian principles? What does this letter teach about the nature of the Christian revolution of society? How should we apply the principles of the letter to the Ephesians and the practice of the letter to Philemon in our own generation? Upon what should our Christian fellowship be based?

CONCLUSION

How did Philemon react to this letter? We do not know for sure, but the fact that the letter was not destroyed indicates that Philemon did what Paul asked. Some feel that the very nature and impact of the letter left Philemon no choice but to send Onesimus back to Paul to whom he meant so much. If this was so, Onesimus no doubt grew as a Christian in fellowship and service with the Apostle Paul.

Some fifty years after this incident, the name of Onesimus appears in church history in letters by Ignatius before his martyrdom. Ignatius speaks of Onesimus, the wonderful bishop of Ephesus. Can this be the runaway slave who gave his life to Jesus Christ in Rome through a prisoner named Paul?

PRACTICAL ACTION

For the sake of obedience to Christ, Onesimus was asked to go back and face the consequences of his former misdeeds. Philemon was asked to sacrifice his pride, to go against social custom and popular opinion in order to forgive his former slave and receive him as a Christian brother. What sacrifice will you make this week because you obey Jesus Christ in all your relationships?